The Jesse Tree for Families

THE JESSE TREE FOR FAMILIES

COLLEEN PRESSPRICH

ILLUSTRATED BY AMY HEYSE

Our Sunday Visitor
Huntington, Indiana

Copyright © 2023 by Colleen Pressprich
28 27 26 25 24 23   1 2 3 4 5 6 7 8 9

Our Sunday Visitor Publishing Division
Our Sunday Visitor, Inc.
200 Noll Plaza
Huntington, IN 46750
1-800-348-2440

ISBN: 978-1-68192-944-6 (Inventory No. T2680)
1. JUVENILE NONFICTION—Holidays & Celebrations—Christmas & Advent.
2. JUVENILE NONFICTION—Religion—Devotional & Prayer.
3. RELIGION—Christianity—Catholic.
LCCN: 2023933776

Cover design: Tyler Ottinger
Interior design: Amanda Falk
Cover and interior art: Amy Heyse

PRINTED IN TURKEY

INTRODUCTION

Growing up in a family that was only culturally Catholic, I never celebrated Advent as its own season. Our Christmas preparations, though joyful, were largely secular. My first introduction to the Jesse Tree came as an adult, when I was working as an assistant in a children's house (a classroom for three- to six-year-olds) at a Christian Montessori school. While researching ways to celebrate Advent in the classroom, I stumbled upon the Jesse Tree and was intrigued. I have loved it ever since.

What Is a Jesse Tree?

Put quite simply, the Jesse Tree is a family tree, more specifically, the family tree of Christ. In it we find the story of how God worked throughout human history in order to bring His children back to Him after the fall.

You can find these family trees depicted in medieval paintings and stained-glass windows throughout Europe. Dating back to the Middle Ages, when most people were illiterate and Bibles were a rare commodity, theologians and priests used art to tell the story of salvation. Many of these family trees began with Jesse, the father of King David, because of the prophecy found in Isaiah 11:1, which states, "But a shoot shall spring from the stump of Jesse, / and from his roots a bud shall blossom." The verse refers to the coming of the Messiah from the family of King David. Over time it became tradition to review the family of Christ each Advent as a way of showing how Jesus fit into the story of the Old Testament.

While we might be familiar with pieces of their stories, the men and women included in Jesus' family tree aren't always who we'd expect. Many would assume that the lineage of the Messiah would be full of kings, the wealthy, the powerful, and those with clear, royal, or unblemished bloodlines. Instead, over and over again we find outsiders, men and women who didn't quite fit — the outcast, the rebel, the not-quite-so-honest — all have their place in the story of salvation. For me, returning to the Jesse Tree each Advent is an opportunity to dig a little deeper into their stories and, as a result, my own. I have found that the better I know the members of the family of Jesus, flawed as they are, the more open I am to the possibility that God might be seeking to work within my own flawed life — which, of course, He is.

This Book's Format

Catholics and Protestants alike use Jesse Trees of all shapes, sizes, and formats to teach children about salvation history during the season of Advent. But even though this tradition has been around for centuries, it is still new to many of us, especially those of us who may not have been raised in devout homes ourselves.

Our family has used many different versions of the Jesse Tree over the years, but we have never settled on one because we never found one that was the right fit: a Catholic Jesse Tree that was accessible to young children but suitable for older kids, too. The book you hold in your hands is my solution to that problem.

In thinking about what would grab my own children's attention in a Jesse Tree book, I realized that the answer was simple. It's the same thing that always captivates them in stories: people and relationships. Children are very relational. Their world is small and people-focused; in fact, it is primarily family-focused. In order to engage my own children, I knew I needed to center this telling of salvation history on the people and families of the stories. As a result, you'll find that each day of this book is focused on a person, and the illustration that goes alongside the meditation is a portrait.

December 1–16

You and your child will explore men and women from both the Old and New Testaments — all people who helped bring God's plan for a Savior to fruition. Each daily reflection is a moment in time with a different member of Jesus' family. It provides a snapshot — a window into the person's character and the way God worked in his or her life. Many of these people lived long and storied lives, and I hope that these vignettes will make your children curious, so they will want to know all about these incredible men and women of faith.

Conversation starters are included with each daily reflection. The goal of these is to help you talk with your child about these stories and grow in faith together. At the back of the book, you'll find a section for parents that contains notes, tips, and scriptural references to help answer any questions you or your children might have.

December 17–24

At this point in Advent, we will switch our focus fully to Jesus and prepare for His coming by learning more about His identity and relationship to His people. To do this, we will dive into another great liturgical tradition of the

Church: the O Antiphons. The O Antiphons have been sung within the Church since the eighth century. They are part of the Divine Office, traditionally recited or sung before Mary's Magnificat during Evening Prayer on the eight days leading up to Christmas. The Divine Office, or Liturgy of the Hours, is prayed by priests, religious, and lay people throughout the Church. Each O Antiphon is a title for Jesus that comes from the Book of Isaiah. For these days, we will use a modified version of *lectio divina* to dive into what these passages tell us about who Christ is and what that means for our lives.

How to Use This Book

Just as there are many different versions of the Jesse Tree, there are many different ways to practice this tradition within your family. There is no right or wrong way, and you may find that your method changes as your family grows and develops its own unique rhythm of family prayer.

Here are a few things that have worked for my family over the years. I share them in hopes that they will inspire your family to create its own rituals. This book is meant to be a guide, a help along your journey of faith. Please feel free to use the ideas that work for your family, but do not feel bound to keep what doesn't.

When to Read This Book Each Day

For my family, anchoring family prayer time to other activities helps to keep us consistent. During Advent, we center our Advent traditions around the dinner table. We have found it to be one of the easiest times of day to consistently gather everyone together, including my husband. We light our Advent wreath and pray our Advent prayers. Then we do our Jesse Tree meditation. The conversation starters often become topics for discussion during the meal.

If your kids don't have the attention span to do this before they eat, then some other options might be reading the meditations during breakfast or making them a part of your bedtime routine. Whichever time you choose, I suggest that you keep it consistent each day of Advent. This will aid you in elevating your Jesse Tree from a routine to a ritual.

A Physical Tree

Many families will use their Christmas tree or a smaller tree or branch alongside the Jesse Tree meditations, hanging an ornament for each day. Our family likes to do this because it marks the passage of time through the month of December in a concrete way — the more ornaments on the tree, the closer we are to the birth of the Savior.

Included with this book (both on the jacket and in a separate section at the back), you'll find a set of ornaments that can be cut out and used each day to mark your journey toward Christmas.

Why Rituals Are Important

Though on the surface they may appear to be similar, routines and rituals arise out of different attitudes and motivations. Routines are often described as those rote activities that we do at the same time in the same way each day. Like routines, rituals are also activities done in the same way time and again, but each word and action is endowed with special meaning and purpose.

The Catholic Church is great at rituals. In a world that is constantly changing, the steadfastness of the Church allows us the comfort of knowing what to expect. I know that during Advent, my pastor will be decked out in purple (except for Gaudete Sunday, when he might wear rose). I can walk into Mass anywhere in the world and recognize the patterns of the words and actions of the priest and congregation in a way that allows me to enter into prayer no matter the language.

Rituals are important to children because this soothing consistency helps them to internalize information more easily. When children do not have to wonder or worry about what comes next, they are able to focus more deeply on content. My husband and I have found that establishing rituals has been crucial to helping faith stick with our kids.

A Final Note on Content

All the reflections contained in this book are appropriate to read even with your youngest family members. These daily meditations are snapshots that focus on an important moment in the life of the individual from Jesus' family tree. I hope that they whet your (and your children's) appetite for more.

For those who are curious, at the end of each reflection I have included information for where in the Bible you can find the person's whole story. However, many of the figures in Jesus' family tree are complicated men and women. I recommend reading the story first yourself before sharing the full biblical account of their lives with your children. Depending on the age and sensitivity of your children, you might find that the version contained in a children's Bible is a better fit.

Introduction for Kids

It's almost Christmas! As we wait and get ready for this special day, we're going to take some time each day to learn about the people in Jesus' family tree. A family tree is a family history. Your family tree includes your siblings, parents, aunts and uncles, cousins, grandparents, great-grandparents, and even great-great-grandparents.

One of the reasons Jesus came to earth was to adopt us, to make us part of His family. This means that when we read the Bible and learn about the men and women in Jesus' family tree — His cousins, parents, aunts and uncles, great-grandparents, great-great-grandparents, and even great-great-great-great grandparents — we are learning about our own family, too.

As we prepare for Christmas, we will read about special people from Jesus' family. We will learn about who they were and how God worked in their lives. And each day we will add an ornament to our Jesse Tree. The more ornaments on our tree, the closer we will be to the birth of Jesus!

Why Do We Do This Each Advent?

Advent is the perfect time to learn about Jesus' family tree because during Advent we are preparing for Jesus' birth at Christmas. In the story of the generations who came before Jesus, we can see how God was preparing the world for His Son.

Why Do We Call It a Jesse Tree?

The special tree we decorate each Advent is named after a man called Jesse, a holy man of God and the father of King David. The prophet Isaiah, many generations before the birth of Jesus, told the Israelites that "a shoot shall sprout from the stump of Jesse, / and from his roots a bud shall blossom" (Is 11:1). This passage foretold the birth of Jesus and told the Jewish people that the Messiah would come from Jesse's family.

December 1 • Adam and Eve

In the cool of the evening, they walked with God in the garden.

Adam and Eve talked with God, strolling slowly and enjoying each other's company. It was cool and comfortable in the garden. They relaxed, surrounded by beauty, breathing in the aromas of the flowers, listening to the chirping of the birds, comforted by the presence of the One who knew them best.

But then they doubted His love and ate the forbidden fruit. They had to leave the garden. After that, it wasn't so easy to find God, to hear Him, to be with Him, as it had been then. Now, in the cool of the evening, they were exhausted after all their labors. They had no time, no energy for leisurely walks or other kinds of pleasure. Most of all, they missed their Creator deeply.

You can read more of Adam and Eve's story in Genesis, beginning in chapter 3.

Note for Parents

When they heard the sound of the LORD God walking about in the garden at the breezy time of the day,
the man and his wife hid themselves from the LORD God among the trees of the garden. — Genesis 3:8

There is nothing like being a parent to make you ponder the Fall of man.

It is instinctual for us as humans to run and hide when we've done something wrong. I first began to notice this tendency when our eldest was about six. She knew when she had done something wrong, often in the very moment when she chose it. Whether it was an impulsive smack to her brother as they argued or a snatched toy, most of the time she didn't need me to tell her that she made a wrong choice.

What she most needed from me was help learning what to do next. Much like Adam and Eve, she was beginning to feel shame and guilt, and these new emotions were unsettling for her. Her instinct was to run and hide from them, both literally and figuratively. She never responded well to raised voices, and she needed the quiet, calm voice of her mother to call her out of the shame and into a position where she could take responsibility for her actions and move forward.

Apart from being a disciplinary matter, this, like so many other matters in child-rearing, has an important spiritual component. How will my children ever learn to run toward God when they are in trouble, if I don't first teach them to run to me and their father? This daunting thought has kept me awake nights in prayer.

I always thought that the ability to run straight to Jesus after sin was purely a gift of grace, but now I'm realizing that there is another piece, one that I am responsible for as my children's mother. We as parents are meant to teach our children to respond to grace. We are their first impression of unconditional love. We give them their first taste of the goodness of the Lord. Part of my job as a mom is to teach my children how to be receptive to grace and how to run into Jesus' arms.

If I can show them how to come to me when they make mistakes, they will unlearn the habit of hiding from shame and guilt. Hopefully this will also pave the way for going to confession down the road, making it second nature.

I am reminded of Saint Thérèse, a favorite intercessor of mine. Her childlike faith has always astounded me and called me higher in my own faith journey. I often meditate on two quotes from her as I help my children learn the value of virtue and discipline without breaking the will God gave them:

You make me think of a little child that is learning to stand but does not yet know how to walk. In his desire to reach the top of the stairs to find his mother, he lifts his little foot to climb the first stair. It is all in vain, and at each renewed effort he falls. Well, be this little child: through the practice of all the virtues, always lift your little foot to mount the staircase of holiness, but do not imagine that you will be able to go up even the first step! No, but the good God does not demand more from you than good will. From the top of the stairs, He looks at you with love. Soon, won over by your useless efforts, He will come down himself and, taking you in His arms, He will carry you up. … But if you stop lifting your little foot, He will leave you a long time on the ground.

Most of all, I follow the example of Mary Magdalene, my heart captivated by her astonishing, or rather loving audacity, which so won the heart of Jesus. It is not because I have been preserved from mortal sin that I fly to Jesus with such confidence and love; even if I had all the crimes possible on my conscience, I am sure I should lose none of my confidence. Heartbroken with repentance, I would simply throw myself into my Savior's arms, for I know how much He loves the Prodigal Son.

I try to remember to keep my voice gentle and even, to listen fully and try to understand the intentions behind my children's actions. When I need to reprimand, I do, but from a place of love, not anger (sometimes this means taking a beating and saying a Hail Mary in my head). I try my best to use natural consequences and to talk with my children about how their actions have affected me or the other members of the family. We talk through ways they can make amends, and then they make the choice. There is usually a snuggle involved. And always, always, I remind them that they are loved no matter what they've done, and that I will be there to help them if they are in trouble.

Do I fail at this? Often. But I am also trying to remember to be like Thérèse and to run into Jesus' arms when I do. I ask forgiveness and for more grace to love more fully and more deeply this family He has given me.

Conversation Starters

- How do you think Adam and Eve felt the day they had to leave the garden?

- How do you feel when you make a mistake or give in to temptation?

- How do you think God felt when He watched Adam and Eve leave the garden?

December 2 • Noah

"Build an ark," God had said. Noah heard His voice loud and clear.

It sounded crazy. They didn't live anywhere near the ocean, and he was no fisherman. But Noah knew that voice, and he knew God. So he built an ark, following the detailed instructions God gave him. Then, without hesitation, he loaded his family and all the animals on board when God told him to.

It took a tremendous amount of work, building that ark. Not to mention the long, sweaty days trying to corral the animals into pens on board! The noise! The smells! Sometimes Noah didn't think he could take it.

Sometimes Noah didn't think he could take the way his neighbors treated him, either. They thought he was foolish, and they told him so. The strangers he could ignore, but men he worked with? Friends he loved? Their mockery was harder to bear.

But Noah knew that voice, and he knew God. So he built an ark.

For forty days, Noah and his family sat in the ark, listening to the sounds of the pounding rain outside flooding the earth. For countless days after the rain stopped, they waited patiently for the water to dry up.

Now, they were back on dry ground. Noah looked at the clouds. No longer a gray blanket stretching from horizon to horizon, these were fluffy and white. They parted to make space for the sun. How he loved the sight of the sun! He tipped his head up, allowing the warmth to touch his face. God was good.

He looked over his shoulder to where the ark stood, on dry ground once again, and then back to the sky. Suddenly, he heard God's voice again, saying, "See, I am now establishing my covenant with you and your descendants after you and with every creature that was with you" (Gn 9:9–10). In the sky appeared a dazzling rainbow, the tangible sign of God's promise.

A slow smile spread over Noah's face. Joy bubbled up from deep within him. His great, rolling laughter echoed in the hills.

You can read more of Noah's story in Genesis, beginning in chapter 6.

Note for Parents

> *So the* Lord *said: I will wipe out from the earth the human beings I have created, and not only the human beings, but also the animals and the crawling things and the birds of the air, for I regret that I made them. But Noah found favor with the* Lord. *— Genesis 6:7–8*

The story of Noah's ark is one of the most well-known and well-loved of all the Bible stories. Most children have heard it before, and most are familiar with the imagery of the rainbow. If your children fall into that category, this is a great day to talk to them about what it means to know God's voice.

Recognizing God's voice and being willing to listen to it set Noah apart from all the other members of the human race during his time. It's also what will set your children apart from many of their peers. Teaching our kids how to hear God is a huge task, but there are simple ways to approach it.

By reading and studying the Bible together, you are helping your children familiarize themselves with God's voice and the different ways He speaks to His people. The Bible is not like other books. As the word of God, it is alive. It has the power to take root in our hearts and speak directly to us. When reading Bible stories with your children, take the time to ask them questions (today's conversation starters can help!). It's a great way to help them to relate to the text and see what God is saying and what it means in their lives.

If you have time today, share a time from your own life when you heard God's voice and listened. It doesn't have to be a big story or even a complicated one; in fact, the simpler the better.

As an example, here's a story from my life that I tell my children:

> One day, back when I used to be a nanny, I was driving to pick up the kids I took care of from school. The whole drive I felt like God was poking me on the shoulder and asking me to stop and get some flowers at the store. That seemed very silly to me. But I kept hearing the Holy Spirit's quiet voice in my head, so I listened and bought the most beautiful bouquet of pink Gerber daisies and went back on my way. When I arrived, I heard that voice again! He was pointing out a woman in the crowd, someone I didn't know, and telling me that I should give the flowers to her! I said NO, at first. But God kept asking, so eventually I gave up and got out of my car. I tapped on the woman's shoulder. She started crying right away when I explained that God had asked me to bring her flowers. It turns out that she had been praying about something very important and asked God for a sign that He heard her.

The follow-up question that I usually get from my kids (and the reason I tell them this story) is, "How did you know that it was God's voice?" I tell my kids that I learned to hear God's voice the same way they are going to learn: I read the Bible to begin to understand what He was like. I started to journal so I could keep track of the words that stuck out to me. I prayed with other people to make sure I was hearing God correctly. That last part is very important. We need to pray with other people! Let this be an opening to begin praying with your children, if that's not something you do already. It's important for them to learn how to hear God's voice from a trusted guide so they won't be steered wrong.

CONVERSATION STARTERS

- How do you think Noah learned how to recognize God's voice?

- How do you think Noah and his family felt while they were in the ark? How do you think you would have felt?

- How do you think they felt when they saw the rainbow?

December 3 • Abraham

Abraham looked up at the sky with its blanket of stars. It comforted him.

Even in his old age, his back bent with the weight of one hundred years on the earth, he still came out each night to remind himself of the promise. Seeing the myriad of stars, the wide expanse, he remembered God's voice. "I will make of you a great nation, and I will bless you" (Gn 12:2), God had told him.

Some days it was difficult to trust that what God said would come true. It had been many years since the Lord had promised him a son, promised to make his descendants as numerous as the stars in the sky. So much had happened since then. At times, he had almost lost faith. Waiting did not come easily to Abraham. So many times he had wanted the promise NOW. So many times he wondered why it was taking so long. And yet God had been faithful, always close at hand, reminding Abraham of His promise, of His goodness, of His love and protection.

In the darkness, a baby cried. Abraham marveled to hear the sound. He spoke a prayer of thanksgiving to the God he knew was with him and went into the tent to meet his new son.

You can read more of Abraham's story in Genesis, beginning in chapter 12.

Note for Parents

> *Some time afterward, the word of the* LORD *came to Abram in a vision: Do not fear, Abram! I am your shield; I will make your reward very great.*
>
> *But Abram said, "Lord GOD, what can you give me, if I die childless and have only a servant of my household, Eliezer of Damascus?" Abram continued, "Look, you have given me no offspring, so a servant of my household will be my heir." Then the word of the* LORD *came to him: No, that one will not be your heir; your own offspring will be your heir. He took him outside and said: Look up at the sky and count the stars, if you can. Just so, he added, will your descendants be. Abram put his faith in the* LORD*, who attributed it to him as an act of righteousness.* — Genesis 15:1–6

There is a well-known saying that when we pray for it, God doesn't give us patience; rather, He gives us the opportunities to practice this valuable virtue. Reading Abraham's story, I have to wonder if he had ever prayed for patience, because boy did he get the opportunity to practice it in spades.

Sometimes, reading the story of Abraham, we can find ourselves skipping ahead from God's promise to Abraham to the moment of Isaac's birth and forget the decades in between. It's easy for us, knowing the outcome, to forget the amount of patience and perseverance in faith it would have taken Abraham (and his wife, Sarah) to continue trusting year after year. The lesson of Abraham's life is as much about Abraham's walk of faith as it is about God's faithfulness to His promises.

If you haven't read the part of Genesis that contains the middle of Abraham's life, I would encourage you to take some time to do it. I think you'll be surprised by all the miles walked, the years endured, and the adventures had.

What stands out to me the most is the way that Abraham maintained a close relationship with the Lord throughout his life. The two didn't part ways after God's promise.

Instead, God kept speaking, and Abraham kept listening. The closer we are to God, the more time we spend conversing with Him, the easier it is to trust Him while we are waiting.

In his Wednesday audience on January 23, 2013, Pope Benedict XVI said of Abraham's choice to trust in the Lord: "How would we have responded to such an invitation? In fact it meant setting out with no directions, no knowledge of where God would lead him; it was a journey that demanded radical obedience and trust, to which faith alone gives access. Yet the dark unknown — to which Abraham had to go — was lit by the light of a promise; God added to his order a reassuring word that unfolded to Abraham a future, life in fullness."

Sometimes parenting can feel a little bit like setting out on an unknown journey. When my children were born, I could not have imagined the people that they would become, could not have foreseen either the gifts and talents they would be blessed with or the struggles that they would have. When my husband and I chose to be open to life, we said yes to God in a very radical way. Abraham's story reminds me that this yes needs to be said over and over again, each and every day, as we are confronted with new stages of development. Abraham's story also reminds me that while God's timeline is often not mine, His faithfulness and love endure. In the difficult seasons of parenting, in the times when everything seems to be a struggle, Abraham stands as a beacon of hope.

Conversation Starters

- How do you think Abraham felt the day after he heard God's promise?

- What do you think made him trust God even when he couldn't see any proof?

- Has it ever been difficult for you to be patient? How can God help you in the waiting?

December 4 • Isaac

Isaac knew he was beloved in the depths of his being.

His mother and father often told him the story of his birth. God had promised them a son and descendants that outnumbered the stars.

Isaac knew that his father, Abraham, was very faithful to the Lord. Isaac tried to follow in his footsteps. He worked hard to be helpful and take care of his parents, because he loved them. So this morning, when his father told him they were going up the mountain to make a sacrifice to God, he went willingly, carrying the bundle of wood that was too heavy for his father.

On the way, Isaac realized that they hadn't brought an animal with them. Worrying that his father was getting forgetful, he asked about it. With averted eyes and a strange tone in his voice, Abraham told him that the Lord would provide an animal for the sacrifice. That was certainly strange. But Isaac trusted his father and continued walking.

When they arrived at the top of the mountain, they laid the wood on the altar. There was still no sign of an animal. Isaac was confused when his father approached him with tears flowing down his face and tied his hands with a rope. Was *he* going to be the sacrifice? What did this mean? Isaac's mind was racing, but his heart was calm and still. He knew his father loved him. He knew his father trusted God. Hadn't his father always taught him that God's ways are not our ways?

Then they heard an angelic voice calling out to them to stop. Isaac knew it was more than perfect timing when they noticed a ram stuck in the bushes nearby.

They sacrificed the animal to God and together gave the mountain a new name, one that means "God provides."

You can read more of Isaac's story in Genesis, beginning in chapter 21.

Note for Parents

When they came to the place of which God had told him, Abraham built an altar there and arranged the wood on it. Next he bound his son Isaac, and put him on top of the wood on the altar. Then Abraham reached out and took the knife to slaughter his son. But the angel of the LORD *called to him from heaven, "Abraham, Abraham!" "Here I am," he answered. "Do not lay your hand on the boy," said the angel. "Do not do the least thing to him. For now I know that you fear God, since you did not withhold from me your son, your only one." — Genesis 22:9–12*

As a parent, my first reaction to this story is horror. Why would God want a father to kill his son?

There are many commentaries on this story written by saints and theologians, and I encourage you to find and read some of them. While I'm not an expert, I do want to share what I've learned from this story by praying through it over the years. It contains a very valuable lesson for me as a mother: My children do not belong to me; they are a gift from God, and He has His own plans for their lives. I'm not suggesting that God is going to ask me to sacrifice my children on an altar, but down the road He may ask me to sacrifice my ideas for what their lives should look like and how He is going to work in them.

How would I react if one of my children discerned that God is calling him or her to mission work in a third world country across the globe? Would I joyfully surrender if one of my daughters wanted to join a cloistered order, or would I grieve bitterly over the prospect of not being able to hug her or watch her raise my grandchildren? What if my son wanted to be a priest? Would I be able to accept the fact that his parish obligations would come first?

I don't know the answer to those questions yet, and perhaps I'll never need to, but I hope that I am able to surrender as Abraham did, to trust that God will work wonders that I cannot see or understand, even if what He seems to be asking is a death of what I desire most.

And how do we explain this story to our kids? In my years of reading the stories of the Jesse Tree to students in my classroom and now as a parent, I have found that this story usually elicits fewer questions than adults expect. Young children pretty easily accept the ending of the story — that God of course saved Isaac and why would He have done anything else? Their simple faith makes it all but certain in their minds that all that comes before — Isaac carrying the wood, asking his dad questions, being put on the altar — is a dramatic build-up before the obvious ending, when God saves the boy. He is God. How could He do anything else? This is what I like to focus on with my kids with this story: Of course God wanted Isaac's good, and Isaac of course trusted God and his earthly father.

There are also obvious parallels to the story of Christ that we can explore as well. For a child who is older or particularly empathetic, it is good to ask the question how they think Abraham was feeling during this story. You can then draw them into a conversation about how God the Father felt at having to sacrifice Jesus for our sins.

Conversation Starters

- Do you know what a sacrifice is? Can you think of any sacrifices you can make for God?

- Isaac carried the wood for Abraham. Do you think Isaac did his job cheerfully? Why or why not?

- How can you help family members when they can't do something, like Isaac did for Abraham?

December 5 • Jacob

Everything the day before had gone according to plan. Jacob had sent his children and his wives across the river into Esau's territory, while he himself waited behind, until he was sure he would have the upper hand. There was a time when his brother did not value his birthright as firstborn son, but there was no guarantee that he felt so now. Jacob would not take the risk. He had worked so hard and for so long, always keeping his goals in sight, not letting obstacles knock him off course.

He was close now. He had managed to get free from his father-in-law. His wives and children were safe, as was the wealth he had toiled for. Jacob took risks, but they were always calculated, and he only wagered when he knew he could control the outcome. He had fought many battles, and he always won.

Until now.

He sat on the rock, pain shooting through his hip, thinking about what had just happened.

He had waited until darkness fell so that he could cross the river without being seen. But just as he reached the bank, he was surprised.

Jacob shook his head. No, *surprised* was not the right word. Stunned. *Stunned* was right. He had heard no sound, received no warning. But suddenly, someone threw his entire weight upon him.

And then they were fighting. Jacob struggled to get the mysterious person off him, to regain control over the situation. He did not give up. They fought until the first light of day broke upon them. Jacob kept wrestling, refusing to give in. He demanded a blessing — what he felt was his due. Finally, the mysterious person struck his hip. Yelling in agony, Jacob had to let go.

But then the person spoke and did a very strange thing: He gave Jacob a new name, *Israel*. The person told him he received this name because "you have contended with divine and human beings and have prevailed" (Gn 32:29). And then he disappeared.

Now Jacob sat alone and puzzled. Something had changed inside of him. Somehow, everything was different now.

You can read more of Jacob's story in Genesis, beginning in chapter 25.

Note for Parents

> *Then the man said, "You shall no longer be named Jacob, but Israel, because you have contended with divine and human beings and have prevailed." Jacob then asked him, "Please tell me your name." He answered, "Why do you ask for my name?" With that, he blessed him. — Genesis 32:29–30*

Jacob's early years don't exactly scream "Patriarch of the Chosen People of God." More than a rascal, Jacob is downright dishonest in many of his interactions. And while he acknowledges God, and even has the vision of a ladder ascending to heaven that is most often associated with him, Jacob doesn't seem to see a need for God in his early years.

Young Jacob was the model of a self-reliant man. He planned, he schemed, and he got what he wanted. But that night on the riverbank, something shifted inside of Jacob as he physically wrestled with God. Jacob was beset by an adversary he did not recognize and had not planned for. And instead of recoiling in fear, surrendering, or attempting to flee, Jacob fought. He struggled. He did not give up. And through the struggle Jacob was changed and became a new man.

This is what I want for my children. I want them to have a real, honest-to-goodness encounter with God. It is quite likely that someday my own children will struggle with God. They will experience a heartbreak they did not expect, grapple with a doctrine they do not understand, or struggle with virtue. And in that moment, I hope that they choose to wrestle with the Lord. I hope that, like Jacob, they engage in the struggle. I want them to go to God and not give up until they are changed.

The *Catechism of the Catholic Church* says: "God renews his promise to Jacob, the ancestor of the twelve tribes of Israel. Before confronting his elder brother Esau, Jacob wrestles all night with a mysterious figure who refuses to reveal his name, but he blesses him before leaving him at dawn. From this account, the spiritual tradition of the Church has retained the symbol of prayer as a battle of faith and as the triumph of perseverance" (2573).

Sharing the story of Jacob wrestling with God is an opportunity for me to tell my children that it's OK to have questions. God can handle a struggle. He won't give up on us or let us go. This story is a chance to reassure children — who by their very nature challenge authority and question everything about the world around them — that God isn't afraid of our questions.

I also share, where and when it's appropriate for their ages and faith stages, some of my own struggles with the Lord. This doesn't mean that I share with them every mistake I've made or every time I've questioned God's will, but I want them to know that my faith is a living faith, one that is growing and developing just like theirs is.

The world tells us that sharing such struggles is a sign of weakness, but I disagree. I want to make sure that my children see me as someone who will not judge their struggles, but rather, will walk with them through the hard times.

CONVERSATION STARTERS

- What do you think of Jacob?

- Who do you think the person was that Jacob wrestled with?

- Jacob felt that somehow, everything was different now. What do you think that means? Why did he feel that way?

December 6 • Joseph

Looking out over the hot desert sands of Egypt, Joseph felt God's presence. It calmed him despite the flutters in his stomach.

His brothers had arrived!

He hadn't seen them since he was a boy. They had hated him then, had stolen his beautiful coat and sent him off with strangers. They had been jealous of him. Their father had given him a beautiful coat, and they hated it because it was a symbol of the fact that their father loved him most. So they had hurt him.

How scared he had been when the strange men had snatched him up and taken him away! His brothers just watched. No one tried to help him when he screamed. After a long and arduous journey, they had arrived in Egypt.

Joseph had no choice then. He had to start a new life. Yet he knew that God walked with him. That made the many years easier, though he still missed his family. He had felt God with him then, just like he did now.

Would his brothers recognize him? What would they think to see him in charge of the whole storehouse of Egypt?

God had protected him and made him prosper. Now Joseph had the chance to use the bad that had been done to him for good. Joseph said a prayer of gratitude to God for helping him feed his family.

Then he took a deep breath and went to hug his brothers.

You can read more of Joseph's story in Genesis, beginning in chapter 37.

Note for Parents

> *I am your brother Joseph, whom you sold into Egypt. But now do not be distressed, and do not be angry with yourselves for having sold me here. It was really for the sake of saving lives that God sent me here ahead of you. The famine has been in the land for two years now, and for five more years cultivation will yield no harvest. God, therefore, sent me on ahead of you to ensure for you a remnant on earth and to save your lives in an extraordinary deliverance. — Genesis 45:4–7*

This story was my favorite tale in my children's Bible growing up, and I asked my nana to read it to me over and over and over again. That time I spent snuggled on her lap listening to the word of God made me a firm believer in the importance of setting the stage with my kids when it comes to faith. My nana helped form a connection in my subconscious between the love that she and I shared and the Bible. It's stayed with me ever since, and it's something that I want for my own children. To that end, I make sure that religion lessons happen in a comfy chair, not at a desk or table. I want them to see the Faith not as an academic subject but as an integral, positive part of their life.

The story of Joseph is the story of a family, of sibling jealousies, and of the way God can heal even after many years. It's a story that speaks of hope and redemption, and it is a great opportunity to discuss sibling rivalry and forgiveness. The thing that had always struck me about Joseph as a child, and that I always try to point out to my own kids now, is that Joseph didn't wallow. He didn't get mad and resentful, even though his brothers sold him into slavery. Instead, he looked to the future and was open to seeing God move in his life in unexpected ways. And he forgave. The truth is that sometimes people hurt us. Sometimes they don't treat us the way we deserve. But we get to choose what happens next.

Teaching my children this lesson early is important to me, because the truth is that there will be people in their lives (though hopefully not their own siblings) who treat them poorly, who wound them or dismiss them. I want my kids to know that even in those moments God can move, not to discount their pain or hurts, but to help them not be held captive by the actions of others.

Though the main theme of this story is forgiveness, one of the things I love about it is that it separates forgiveness from reconciliation. In the modern world, we often put the two together and assume that reconciliation must be a part of forgiveness. But in this story, we see that though Joseph and his brothers are indeed reconciled in the end, the forgiveness came long before. Joseph didn't let what his brothers had done to him color his life. He forgave them long before they arrived in Egypt asking for help.

This is an important distinction, because the truth is that forgiveness only requires us, and is within our power, but reconciliation requires both parties. We are called to forgive all who harm us, but we are not called to be reconciled with everyone. When we teach our children to forgive, we aren't asking them to be doormats. Yes, we are asking them to courageously let go of anger and hardness of heart, but we need to remember to give them space to discern (where age appropriate) whether reconciliation should follow after that forgiveness. Sometimes it's not prudent (or safe or healthy) to continue in a friendship or a relationship even after we have forgiven someone. In my own life, I have found that when I separate the two in my mind and heart, I find it much easier to offer forgiveness as Christ asks of me.

Conversation Starters

- Do you ever feel jealous like Joseph's brothers?

- How do you think Joseph felt when he was in Egypt, away from his family?

- Why do you think Joseph forgave his brothers? Do you think you could have if you were in his shoes?

December 7 • Moses

I AM Who AM.

Moses repeated the words over and over to himself. The remembrance of them gave him courage. They were the words God spoke to him from within the burning bush — the words that changed his life.

He did not feel ready for this moment now, standing before Pharoah. When he was nervous, he stuttered. He was nervous now. Why had God chosen him for this task? Couldn't He have chosen someone better? Someone stronger, who could speak clearly? A leader?

He was glad to have his brother, Aaron, with him in Pharoah's throne room. The Lord was so good to give him that help! Aaron spoke when Moses couldn't; Aaron, along with their sister, Miriam, convinced the Israelites to believe what Moses said.

What if the Pharaoh didn't listen to his words? What if the Israelite people decided they didn't want him to lead them to freedom after all? He was a stranger to most of them, hardly the person they would have chosen as their leader.

I AM Who AM.

The words echoed in his head and heart. Moses felt peace warming his body like the rays of the sun.

He raised his head and straightened his back. Calm and collected, he met Pharoah's eyes and announced, "Thus says the Lord, the God of Israel: Let my people go" (Ex 5:1).

You can read more of Moses' story in Exodus, beginning in chapter 2.

Note for Parents

> *But Moses said to God, "Who am I that I should go to Pharaoh and bring the Israelites out of Egypt?" God answered: I will be with you; and this will be your sign that I have sent you. When you have brought the people out of Egypt, you will serve God at this mountain. "But," said Moses to God, "if I go to the Israelites and say to them, 'The God of your ancestors has sent me to you,' and they ask me, 'What is his name?' what do I tell them?" God replied to Moses: I am who I am. Then he added: This is what you will tell the Israelites: I AM has sent me to you. — Exodus 3:11–14*

Like many of the well-known stories of the Old Testament, the tale of Moses can be easy to gloss over. We already know how it ends: Moses frees the Israelites and leads them out of slavery in Egypt. Moses looms large in biblical history, a gigantic figure.

But Moses wasn't always Moses. If you would have asked the Israelites who they would choose as their leader, it probably wouldn't have been him. In fact, he'd been rejected by his people before, earlier in his life.

For most of his early life, Moses was an outsider. Moses was raised as a prince of Egypt by Pharaoh's daughter. While he knew he was an Israelite and sometimes ventured among them, he didn't live with his people or share their back-breaking work. Even after Moses had stepped in, killing an Egyptian who was beating a Hebrew man, the Israelites made it clear that they didn't want him meddling in their affairs. Moses subsequently ended up fleeing to Midian with a price on his head. He married a Midianite woman and built a life there.

Moses also had a stutter, so he was terrified to speak in public. That's why God allowed his brother, Aaron, to accompany him on his mission and speak for him.

Moses wasn't the bravest, the fastest, the most handsome, the most popular, or the most eloquent. He had a quick temper, and sometimes he made terrible mistakes. In short, Moses was not the clear choice for a leader.

But God chose him anyway. And that is hope for all of us who aren't the fastest, most handsome, most popular, most whatever. God saw Moses for the entirety of who he was and chose him despite his flaws. His story is an opportunity to encourage our children to look past appearances and first impressions when they meet other people. We learn from Moses' story to treat everyone with kindness and respect, as children of God.

The story of Moses shows us someone with a disability, and yet the disability didn't define him or keep him from doing God's will; it was just one part of him.

The story of Moses also shows a strong relationship between siblings. Moses, Aaron, and Miriam occasionally argue, and there are jealousies and bickering in their relationship that will ring true to any set of siblings today, but the strongest thread in their story is love. Miriam is instrumental in saving Moses' life as a baby. Time and again Aaron, the older brother, immediately steps up when Moses needs him. Aaron and Miriam helped get the Israelites on board with having Moses as their leader. Aaron, knowing his brother's struggle with public speaking, goes with him to speak to Pharoah. He does not lord his own gifts over his brother or make him feel like less; he simply walks alongside him, being of help where he can.

Without his brother and sister, Moses would not have succeeded in becoming the man God destined him to be. The lesson here is that God gives us families to walk beside us, to help us along our journies of faith.

Conversation Starters

- How do you think you would have felt if you were in Moses' place?

- How do you think Aaron felt?

- What do you think made Aaron agree to help his brother?

December 8 • Rahab

Rahab had heard all the stories. As innkeeper she spoke with all the travelers who came through Jericho. And lately, all the news centered around one thing: the destruction that the Israelites left in their wake. From her perch from within the city walls, she could see that the tales she had heard were true. The Israelites were indeed an intimidating army.

But while the king and his men were focused on fortifying the city walls and arming the people inside, Rahab knew the truth: It wasn't the men below they had to fear; it was their God. The God of the Israelites had killed all the firstborn of the Egyptians in a single night. He had drowned Pharaoh's army in the Red Sea. He leveled cities and laid claim to nations. It was He who held the power.

But Rahab had heard other stories about this mysterious God as well — how He fed His people in the desert so they never went hungry. How He traveled before and behind them so they didn't get lost. How He had given them laws so they would know how to stay close to Him. This was a new kind of God to her — one who cared, one who protected, one who loved.

Rahab yearned to be a part of this God's people, and not just because she was sure He would win the battle to come, though she knew He would. No, stronger than her desire to be safe from harm was her longing to be cared for, protected, loved.

Clear-sighted and bold, Rahab wasn't going to let her chance slip by. She knew the two strangers who had walked into her inn several days ago were spies. She offered them a chance to escape, but only if they would save her and her family in return. Now she sat at her window, watching the red silk flutter gently in the breeze, watching the approaching army, praying that the men she had saved would be faithful. She hoped for a future with this God of the Israelites.

You can read more of Rahab's story in the Book of Joshua, beginning in chapter 2.

Note for Parents

"Now then, swear to me by the Lord *that, since I am showing kindness to you, you in turn will show kindness to my family. Give me a reliable sign that you will allow my father and mother, brothers and sisters, and my whole family to live, and that you will deliver us from death." "We pledge our lives for yours," they answered her. "If you do not betray our mission, we will be faithful in showing kindness to you when the* Lord *gives us the land."*

Then she let them down through the window with a rope; for she lived in a house built into the city wall. — Joshua 2:12–15

In every passage of the Bible where Rahab is mentioned by name (save one), she is known by the moniker "Rahab the Harlot." She was an innkeeper, yes, but in the time and place where she lived, she would have almost certainly been a prostitute as well. And that was how the world she lived in defined her — by her profession, with derision. She was useful, but not valued, desired, or loved.

And yet, she was chosen. Her name stands with the others in Matthew's lineage of Christ, where she is not known by her former profession, but rather as "Rahab, mother of Boaz."

We know very little about Rahab's life either before or after her interactions with Joshua's spies. While there is much in her life that would have been outside of her control, she saw an opportunity and she seized it with both hands. After risking her life to become one of the Lord's Chosen People, she and her family were spared by the

Israelites, but more than that, they were welcomed into the fold of God's Chosen People.

Through her faith Rahab was redefined, and her life was put on a new path. There is nothing to indicate that she looked back or wallowed in her former sin. Rahab took the escape offered to her and moved past her own past. And if we look at Boaz (who appears in Ruth's story tomorrow), we can see the wonderful job his mother did in raising him.

For myself, Rahab's inclusion in the lineage of Christ reminds me that my past does not dictate my future. This is a reminder that I find I need regularly, especially in difficult seasons of life. God's grace is new each morning, and I want to make sure that I am taking full advantage of that.

For my children, I want them to see that Rahab was willing to risk everything to be a part of God's people — a people that they already belong to. I want my kids to see her sacrifice and think, "Wow, I am so blessed to already be a member of God's family." Rahab's story is an opportunity for me to talk to my children about the privilege that they have by virtue of their baptism. Not every child is born into a home that will teach them about Jesus. Not every child is given the gift of catechesis, the chance to learn the Scriptures, or even the opportunity to attend Mass every week. I hope that Rahab's story makes them grateful for the blessings in their faith lives and helps them to treasure them dearly.

Conversation Starters

- What stood out to you in Rahab's story?

- What do you think made her brave enough to betray her king and his soldiers?

- What do you think happens next?

December 9 • Ruth

Do you have to feel brave in order to be brave?

Boaz had told Ruth she was courageous. Truth be told, she didn't always feel that way. She had always been more practical than anything else. She hadn't set out to be courageous when she came to this land with her mother-in-law. She just wanted to care for someone she loved.

When her first husband died, she could have stayed in Moab with her family. It was the only home she had ever known. But her mother-in-law, Naomi, was going to go back to Israel. She would be all alone there with no one to help her or take care of her. Ruth loved Naomi and wouldn't let that happen when she had the power to change it. So she told Naomi, "Where you go, I will go. … Your people shall be my people" (Ru 1:16), and she wouldn't take no for an answer.

They made the long journey back to Israel together. When they arrived, there was no welcome prepared for them, no home to return to. The two women were entirely on their own. They settled in as best they could, and Ruth set about finding a way to provide food for them. Thankfully, Israel had a law that allowed the poor to feed themselves without begging. They were allowed to follow behind the men harvesting grain in the fields, to pick up any pieces that fell to the ground. This was called *gleaning*.

Ruth went every day to glean in the fields. It was hard work, and Ruth's back ached at the end of each day. But it meant that there was food on the table at night. And it meant that Naomi was cared for.

Ruth wasn't sure why Boaz took notice of her, but she was grateful that he did. He was a kind and generous man, and she knew that he had told his men to protect her. He admired her courage. But one day, he would realize that the driving force in her life wasn't bravery, it was love.

You can read more of Ruth's story in the Book of Ruth.

Note for Parents

> But Ruth said, *"Do not press me to go back and abandon you!*
>
> *Wherever you go I will go,*
>   *wherever you lodge I will lodge.*
> *Your people shall be my people*
>   *and your God, my God.*
> *Where you die I will die,*
>   *and there be buried.*
>
> *May the* Lord *do thus to me, and more, if even death separates me from you!" (Ruth 1:16–17)*

Ruth, like Rahab, is one of only four women listed in the genealogy of Jesus that begins the Gospel of Matthew.

Ruth, a Moabite woman, would have been an outcast to the people of Israel, not worthy of notice, not even worthy of being included in society. And having been married to an Israelite man, she likely would have known this when she set out with Naomi. She went nonetheless. Ruth becomes a symbol of faithfulness by declaring to Naomi, "Your God [will be] my God" (Ru 1:16) and then truly (and literally) walking the walk with her back to Naomi's homeland and farther.

Ruth's story is one of courage, a courage rooted in love. Her love for Naomi is what made her leave everything she knew, and it was what sustained her as she started a new life in a new land. She knew that as an elderly woman on her own, Naomi would have struggled, even amongst her own people. Ruth loved Naomi and couldn't leave her on her own.

It is also a story of how the Lord provides, how He welcomes the stranger into the fold, how He grafts new branches onto the vine. That makes this story an encouraging read for those children who find themselves in the position of going somewhere new, of being the person no one recognizes.

This story presents many lessons for how we ourselves treat strangers — whether at school, in our parish, or in our larger community and country. Thinking about how Ruth felt upon her arrival in Israel is a great opportunity for kids to practice putting themselves in a stranger's shoes. My hope for my own children is that they can be like Boaz, and, when confronted by a stranger, look past appearances, nationalities, and socioeconomic status, and see each person for the individual he or she is: a person created in the image and likeness of God.

If you have children with fears in social situations, Ruth is a wonderful patron, someone they can ask for help. Ruth set out to a new land despite her probable trepidation, and when she got there, she very matter-of-factly stepped out to look for work and food — no small feat for a woman in her day. If you were to read the whole of the Book of Ruth (and you should, it's only a few pages long and positively delightful), you'll find that it never once says that Ruth didn't feel afraid. Ruth's quiet example can provide all of us with comfort and strength.

CONVERSATION STARTERS

- How do you think Ruth felt when she left her family to go with Naomi? How do you think she felt when they arrived in Israel?

- How do you think it made Naomi feel to have Ruth with her?

- What do you think gave Ruth her courage?

December 10 • Jesse

Jesse wasn't surprised when he got Samuel's invitation.

He was surprised, though, when Samuel asked him to bring his sons along — all of them. He watched with curiosity as Samuel greeted each one personally. This was unusual. Maybe Samuel wasn't just in Bethlehem for a sacrifice. What was the prophet doing? More importantly, what was the Lord doing?

Samuel stared at each young man. Then he shook his head, and each time he repeated the words, "The LORD has not chosen this one" (1 Sm 16:9). What could Samuel be looking for? Courage? They had it. Strength? None were stronger. Good looks? His boys were the handsomest.

At the end of the line, Samuel turned to Jesse. The question surprised him: "Are these all the sons you have?" (1 Sm 16:11). He had a feeling that the prophet already knew that the answer was no. Because of course, there was David, the youngest, the smallest, the quietest. David, who had been sent to tend the sheep.

Now Jesse watched as Samuel looked over David. David was out of breath, fresh from the fields, smelling like sheep. A smile spread over the prophet's face as he brought out the horn of oil and anointed David's head.

Jesse still didn't understand what God was calling David to do. Yet it was clear he was chosen for a great purpose. Jesse prayed that he would be able to see his boy as God saw him, so that he could help him fulfill his great purpose.

You can read more of Jesse's story in 1 Samuel, beginning in chapter 16.

Note for Parents

[Samuel] also had Jesse and his sons purify themselves and invited them to the sacrifice. As they came, he looked at Eliab and thought, "Surely the anointed is here before the LORD." But the LORD said to Samuel: Do not judge from his appearance or from his lofty stature, because I have rejected him. God does not see as a mortal, who sees the appearance. The LORD looks into the heart. Then Jesse called Abinadab and presented him before Samuel, who said, "The LORD has not chosen him." Next Jesse presented Shammah, but Samuel said, "The LORD has not chosen this one either." In the same way Jesse presented seven sons before Samuel, but Samuel said to Jesse, "The LORD has not chosen any one of these."

Then Samuel asked Jesse, "Are these all the sons you have?" Jesse replied, "There is still the youngest, but he is tending the sheep." Samuel said to Jesse, "Send for him; we will not sit down to eat until he arrives here." Jesse had the young man brought to them. He was ruddy, a youth with beautiful eyes, and good looking. The LORD said: There — anoint him, for this is the one! Then Samuel, with the horn of oil in hand, anointed him in the midst of his brothers, and from that day on, the spirit of the LORD rushed upon David. Then Samuel set out for Ramah. — 1 Samuel 16:5–13

Considering that this Advent tradition bears his name, there is surprisingly little about Jesse's life in the Scriptures, where he is depicted briefly in three episodes of David's life. We know that he was the son of Obed and the grandson of Boaz and Ruth. We can infer a few things from Scripture. First, we know that he owned flocks of sheep, which indicates that he was a man of wealth. We can also assume that, like his grandfather before him, he was a landowner. Based on the treatment he receives from Samuel and King Saul, it is obvious that he was a man of some standing within the community.

Interestingly, much more about his life is found in the Jewish Talmud and Rabbinic tradition. Both tell that

Jesse was not just someone of wealth and consequence but, more importantly, that he was also a holy man. In fact, tradition holds that Jesse was one of only four men to die without sin.

But despite his closeness to God and reputation for holiness, Jesse still didn't see his youngest son as God did. He couldn't understand God's plan for David. For us as parents, this story is a reminder to take a step back, to listen, and to seek to understand the ways that God is working in our children. It's an opportunity to recognize that our children belong to God more than they do to us, and that He knew them before they came to be. He very well might have plans for them beyond what we can imagine. Our role is to help support God's plan for their lives — to love them unconditionally and move over when our will and God's will for them conflict.

CONVERSATION STARTERS

- What do you think David's brothers were thinking and feeling as Samuel looked at them?

- What about when they saw their little brother anointed with holy oil?
- Do you think that Jesse was surprised that Samuel chose David? Why or why not?

- Do you think that Jesse knew what was happening when David was anointed?

December 11 • David

What joy welled up inside his soul as he thought of all that God had done for him! David couldn't contain himself — he just had to move. He joined his people in the street and began to dance. And as he danced, he saw puzzled surprise in the eyes of his subjects. They weren't used to a king behaving this way. Certainly Saul, the old king, never danced!

He knew that some people didn't understand. They didn't know what it felt like to be filled to overflowing with the Spirit of God. David wanted that for his people. He wanted them to know God the way he did. The moment when Samuel had anointed his head all those years ago had changed his life. Not because it had marked him as king, but because at that moment, the Spirit of the Lord had rushed upon him. It was rushing still, a constant movement inside him that overpowered everything else.

He had to dance, had to sing, had to praise this God who overwhelmed him with love. Maybe, just maybe, if his subjects saw him dancing and singing for the Lord without caring what other people thought, they would realize that it is OK to look foolish in front of people if you're doing the right thing in God's eyes.

You can read more of David's story beginning in 1 Samuel 16.

Note for Parents

> *Then David came dancing before the* Lord *with abandon, girt with a linen ephod. David and all the house of Israel were bringing up the ark of the* Lord *with shouts of joy and sound of horn. — 2 Samuel 6:14–15*

David is one of the few people in the Old Testament to experience the same Spirit that the apostles received at Pentecost. The phrasing in the Bible is quite extraordinary: "The spirit of the Lord rushed upon David" (1 Sm 16:13). I love how powerful the verb choice is. It is no wonder that praise and prophecy flowed from his lips like water.

Praising the Lord out loud like David did is still foreign to many of us, but it is incredibly important. When prayer begins with praise, it puts us in the right position before God. Praise allows us to remember that God is God and we are not. It also helps us to grow in intimacy with God, because it moves our focus outside of ourselves.

Just as we build our kids' vocabulary by reading books and using precise words around them, we can build a vocabulary of praise for our kids by using praise out loud in front of them. One of the simplest ways to encourage our children to praise God is to express our own wonder at God's creation. Like David, so many of whose psalms have themes of wonder and awe at what God has done, we can model this for our kids by marveling out loud about the world around us:

- *Wow! Look at that incredible sunset! God, how amazingly creative You are to have decided to mix pink and blue together!*
- *Look at that ladybug's polka dots! I think God must have had so much fun creating all of the different types of bugs, don't you?*
- *Hey, you climbed to a higher branch in the tree than yesterday! It's incredible the way your muscles and brain all work together to help you get up that tree. Thank You, God, for giving William a strong body and the gift of perseverance.*

As we get into the habit of noticing God's hand in the world around us, in all the teeny tiny details of creation, it becomes more and more natural to praise His goodness.

If you are somebody for whom this is new, you could try putting on a praise and worship station in the car or pulling one up on your phone or tablet before you start family prayers. When we do moments of free praise at the start of our family's prayer time, I try to encourage my children to use their own words. But, as any good teacher knows, sometimes it's helpful to have a little scaffolding in a lesson. Perhaps to start out, you can share some common words of praise that they can use: "God, you are my …"; "I love you …"; "Glory to you …"; "Blessed are you …"

You can also use some of God's many beautiful titles: Word-made-Flesh; Holy One of Israel; Font of Holiness; Wonderful Counselor; Adonai; Abba Father; True Vine; Lord of Heaven and Earth; Refuge and Shelter; Father of Lights; Emmanuel (God with us); King of Glory; King of the Universe; Ancient of Days; Merciful Savior; Glorious Messiah; Holy Redeemer; Healer; Lion of Judah; Lord of All; Lord of Hosts; Good Shepherd; Great High Priest; Name Above All Names; Alpha and Omega.

One final note: Like many members of Jesus' family tree, David is a complicated figure. He was a great king and also a man who made great mistakes. The psalms attributed to David are some of the most beautiful and raw parts of the Bible. There is no sugarcoating in David's story, not even when he himself tells it. Older children might be able to handle the fullness of David's story because of how he repented of his horrific sin. As they begin struggling with their own sins, difficulties in life, or even with their relationships with God, they can be introduced to some of his psalms that they might not have seen in a children's Bible. They might find comfort in his brutal honesty about his situation and his emotions.

Conversation Starters

- What do you think it feels like to have the Spirit of God rush upon you?

- Do you think David was surprised?

- Have you ever felt like there was something you wanted to do but you held back because of what other people might think?

December 12 • Solomon

Solomon looked around the camp at the sleeping forms of his men. They were always within reach, always surrounding him. It surprised him to know how lonely one could feel even in the midst of so many people. He was still getting used to that and everything else that came with being a king. But right now, in the dead of night, he was the only one awake. Silently, he sat and pondered the dream that had given him peace.

Since the day he had sat by his dying father's side and listened to his final instructions, Solomon's mind had been full of turmoil. He had not expected to be named king. That should have gone to one of his older brothers. But he had been chosen to carry on his father's legacy, and Solomon wanted to do it well. He didn't want to let his people down. He didn't want to let the Lord down.

Then the Lord appeared to him in a dream. He offered Solomon anything he wanted. Solomon didn't hesitate for a second: He asked for wisdom. Wisdom was what he needed if he was going to be king, if he was going to protect and guide the people of Israel. His answer pleased God, who granted his request. God also promised him riches and renown. How astounding! But Solomon did not want to be distracted by riches or fame. No, the Lord had granted him wisdom, and he would use it to rule his people well.

You can read more of Solomon's story in First Kings, beginning in chapter 1.

Note for Parents

In Gibeon the LORD *appeared to Solomon in a dream at night. God said: Whatever you ask I shall give you. Solomon answered: "You have shown great kindness to your servant, David my father, because he walked before you with fidelity, justice, and an upright heart; and you have continued this great kindness toward him today, giving him a son to sit upon his throne. Now,* LORD, *my God, you have made me, your servant, king to succeed David my father; but I am a mere youth, not knowing at all how to act — I, your servant, among the people you have chosen, a people so vast that it cannot be numbered or counted. Give your servant, therefore, a listening heart to judge your people and to distinguish between good and evil. For who is able to give judgment for this vast people of yours?"*

The Lord was pleased by Solomon's request. — 1 Kings 3:5–10

Time and time again, God challenges our expectations by calling the least likely people to fulfill His designs.

Solomon is the living embodiment of the saying, "God doesn't call the qualified, He qualifies the called." He was not the eldest son of King David, and was not the one many Israelites hoped would take up the throne upon David's death. In fact, another of David's sons was holding a banquet to celebrate his own upcoming kingship at the very moment David anointed Solomon as his heir. It was only through the maneuverings of Bathsheba, Solomon's mother, and Nathan the prophet that Solomon ended up on the throne.

But though he was just a youth, Solomon didn't shrink from the task set before him. And today he is honored in Judaism, Islam, and Christianity not just as a wise king and a just ruler, but as the wisest king in the history of all three religions.

For me as a parent, Solomon's is the story I keep in my back pocket for when my kids compare themselves to others, when they feel like they aren't good enough, or when they think that they don't measure up. The lesson of Solomon is not that you have to be the strongest, smartest, fastest, or best, but rather that you need to follow the calling that God sets before you. Solomon succeeds as a king for two major reasons: first, because he accepts the plan that God has for him and settles into his rightful place; and second, because he turns to God in his need.

Obviously, we as parents know that further along in the story, Solomon falls from grace. He strays from the path that God set out for him and slowly allows worship of foreign gods into his life. This, of course, leads to destruction, not just for him but for all of Israel as well.

If your children are older, they might have already come across this part of Solomon's life. If they have, I would encourage you not to shy away from the topic. Solomon's story can be a wonderful opportunity to talk with your children about the fact that human beings, even epic biblical figures, often sin and fall from grace. Like all of us, Solomon made some wonderful decisions and some very bad ones. It's okay to praise and admire the good he did while also condemning the bad.

This can be a hard thing to do, even for adults. Indeed, it's one of the most beautiful and challenging parts of our Faith: God calls us to believe that anyone can be saved, no matter what they have done. He asks us to extend mercy and forgiveness to others. If this is something you struggle with (perhaps it's something that you are wrestling with God about right now), it's OK to admit that to your children. Remember, they don't need you to be perfect, they just need to see you trying.

Conversation Starters

- How do you think Solomon felt when he was made king?
- What do you think you would ask for if God appeared to you?
- What do you think Solomon did next? What would your first decision as king be?

December 13 • Elizabeth

Elizabeth eased herself into a standing position. She walked slowly around the room to get her blood flowing. Her movements got slower the bigger she got, but Elizabeth didn't mind. Six months of carrying this precious child inside her had taught her more about love and gratitude than she had ever known before.

The Lord had heard her prayer! He had given her a child, even in her old age. What a wonder! What joy! What love! Soon, soon, she and Zechariah would be able to share their good news with the people they loved.

Suddenly behind her she heard a noise. She turned and gasped in surprise. Standing in the doorway was her beloved cousin, Mary. Despite her age and size, Elizabeth moved quickly to greet her.

Their eyes met. In Mary's quiet hello, Elizabeth heard something else: a promise kept, a covenant fulfilled. She felt the baby leap for joy in her womb. Joy welled up inside her. Elizabeth spoke: "Most blessed are you among women, and blessed is the fruit of your womb" (Lk 1:42).

You can read more of Elizabeth's story in Luke, beginning in chapter 1.

Note for Parents

> *When Elizabeth heard Mary's greeting, the infant leaped in her womb, and Elizabeth, filled with the holy Spirit, cried out in a loud voice and said, "Most blessed are you among women, and blessed is the fruit of your womb. And how does this happen to me, that the mother of my Lord should come to me? For at the moment the sound of your greeting reached my ears, the infant in my womb leaped for joy. Blessed are you who believed that what was spoken to you by the Lord would be fulfilled." — Luke 1:41–45*

Today, with our reflection on Elizabeth, we move from the Old Testament to the New. This is a turning point in the Advent season, a moment to reflect on how close we are to the coming of the Messiah. Elizabeth's story also offers a fitting counterpoint to Adam and Eve. In her trust and joy, we find the opposite of their doubt.

Though she appears in only a few scenes of the Gospels, they are rich and full of meaning. Elizabeth is first introduced as a woman filled with the Holy Spirit. She is mentioned alongside her husband, as an equal in holiness and standing before God. Chosen to be the mother of John the Baptist, Elizabeth was a powerhouse of a woman and a mom.

Elizabeth's pregnancy began after her husband, Zechariah, was rendered mute because he questioned the angel who announced it. He didn't speak again until after John's birth. In all likelihood, Elizabeth, like most women of her time, would have been illiterate, making it nearly impossible to communicate to her husband with words. Luke tells us that upon realizing she was pregnant, Elizabeth went into seclusion, navigating the beginning of her pregnancy in quiet trust of the Lord. That time of prayer and preparation ended with the arrival of her cousin Mary.

Precious little is said about their relationship, but Mary's immediately leaving for Elizabeth's home upon hearing the news of both of their pregnancies gives us a clue to the depth of friendship and love between them. When reading Elizabeth's story, the first thing that always stands out to me is how immediate her response to Mary's arrival is. Her bond with both her unborn child and with God is strong — she feels John leap with joy within her and is also illuminated to the reason for that joy. She adds her own joy to his, speaking out loud the good news about the coming of the Messiah — the first human words recorded praising God's Son after His Incarnation.

When I compare this to my own faith, I am left with the recognition that I have a very long way to go before I reach her heights. While I have learned over the years what God's still, small voice sounds like in the quiet of my heart, rarely do I recognize it as instantly as she does. And more rarely still do I respond with my own actions as quickly.

In Elizabeth, I see a woman whose level of faith I aspire to. She is an example of the correct response to God's movement in our lives. This prompts me to be more fervent in my children's faith education, teaching them how to hear God's voice. For my family, this looks like spending time in prayer with our children each morning — prayer time that includes Scripture, the word of God.

The story of the Visitation, which we see from Elizabeth's perspective today, is a wonderful opportunity to talk with your children about the ways that they can bring joy to the people they love. We all have family members and friends who would benefit from a surprise visit, or if that's not possible, a phone call, video chat, or even a card in the mail.

Conversation Starters

- What do you think Mary felt when Elizabeth greeted her?

- Elizabeth wasn't expecting Mary to come, but she felt loved when she arrived. What people in your life might appreciate a visit or a note from you?

December 14 • John the Baptist

The cold water rushed around John's waist as the current tugged at his feet. The sun sparkled off the water. It was a beautiful day.

Suddenly, his heart started beating faster in his chest. John knew what that feeling meant: Jesus was close by. He could always feel his cousin's presence. He had known when Jesus was near since before he was born! At least, that's what his mother told him, and he believed her.

It was a gift, knowing that the Savior walked the earth, but even more than that, it was a responsibility. He knew God's plan for salvation was coming true right now. The Messiah his people had been waiting for was here! The immensity of that knowledge spurred him forward. How many people would need to repent before they could recognize Jesus? John knew that Jesus might not be the Messiah most people expected. Still, he prayed they would come to see who Jesus was.

Day in and day out, he returned to the river, calling the people to change their ways so they would know Jesus when they met Him. Because how could they know their Savior if they were blinded by sin? If their hearts were closed, would they be able to tell the Messiah had arrived?

Today, John was surprised to see Jesus walk right into the river. He wondered what was going to happen next as he embraced his cousin in a tight hug.

Read what happens next in Matthew 3.

Note for Parents

> *John wore clothing made of camel's hair and had a leather belt around his waist. His food was locusts and wild honey. At that time Jerusalem, all Judea, and the whole region around the Jordan were going out to him and were being baptized by him in the Jordan River as they acknowledged their sins. — Matthew 3:4–6*

St. John the Baptist was utterly unabashed to be himself. In Scripture, he is described as wearing clothes made of camel's hair and eating locusts and honey. John certainly stood out, and not just in his choice of outfit and food. His life and his lifestyle all pointed to one thing: The Messiah was coming, and people needed to be ready.

John is an interesting character because he knew Jesus. He knew who Jesus was before anyone else did, with the exception of Joseph and Mary. Catholic tradition tells us that as a child, John knew Christ. This is why he is often depicted in paintings of Mary and the Child Jesus. Think about that. John knew Jesus and got to grow up knowing Jesus — not knowing *about* Him, but really knowing Him.

By the time John grew up, his whole life had been grounded in the knowledge of who Jesus was — and who he was in relationship to Jesus. John lived out his life in confidence, secure in his identity. This is what we want for our own children, but it will only come as a result of their relationship with Christ. If our kids know who God is and know who they are in relationship to Him (beloved sons and daughters), then they will be able to stand firm in the face of the world and not bow to pressure to conform to who society tells them to be.

So how do we accomplish this?

We remember that while Jesus is no longer walking among us as He did in Nazareth two thousand years ago, even to this day He makes himself small and helpless and available to us in the Blessed Sacrament.

The Eucharist is the Christ Child's gift to us in the Church today. Through the Eucharist, our children will find the strength of relationship they need to combat the world's expectations. The miracle of the Eucharist, of Christ being fully present, Body, Blood, Soul, and Divinity in the Host, is not difficult for the faith of children to grasp. Their hearts, still open to wonder, do not find it hard to believe that God wants to be close to us. That He might choose this particular way of drawing close may be confounding to adults, but I have found that children, though often full of questions, do not struggle with this doctrine.

The more we bring our children to Jesus in the Blessed Sacrament, the easier it will be for them to know Him. There are so many ways to do this. A simple habit our family has found fruitful is acknowledging every Catholic church we pass by. Often this means that when my husband or I notice a church while we are walking or in the car, we point it out to the kids, and then we make the Sign of the Cross and call out, "Hello, Jesus, we love You!" The kids usually gleefully follow suit. When we are able to stop, we go in and find the tabernacle, to pay a few moments of homage to God. The children say hello, tell Him about their days, and ask for help if they need it.

CONVERSATION STARTERS

- What do you think it was like for John the Baptist to know that the Messiah had arrived on earth?

- Do you think he ever told anyone? Why? Why not?

- What do you think you would have felt if you were John in the river when Jesus arrived and asked to be baptized?

December 15 • Joseph

Joseph had finally fallen into a deep sleep. It had taken him quite a while to fall asleep that night. The Baby had been awake for a long time! As Joseph slept, he had a dream, and in his dream the angel appeared to him — again. This time, the angel told him to take the Child and His mother to Egypt, because Herod wanted to kill the Baby.

Joseph woke up with a start. He knew that they needed to leave at once. He trusted the angel, who had appeared to him in a dream once before. In the last dream, the angel had told him to take Mary as his wife and to raise Jesus as his Son.

Sometimes, Joseph wondered why Mary didn't receive these dreams. After all, she was the one who gave birth to God himself! Joseph was just a humble carpenter. But it wasn't his place to question whom God chose. It was his place to care for Jesus and Mary.

Joseph stretched and yawned. He reached over to gently shake Mary awake. It was time to leave.

Read Joseph's full story in the Gospel of Matthew, beginning with Chapter 1, verse 18.

Note for Parents

> *Now this is how the birth of Jesus Christ came about. When his mother Mary was betrothed to Joseph, but before they lived together, she was found with child through the holy Spirit. Joseph her husband, since he was a righteous man, yet unwilling to expose her to shame, decided to divorce her quietly. Such was his intention when, behold, the angel of the Lord appeared to him in a dream and said, "Joseph, son of David, do not be afraid to take Mary your wife into your home. For it is through the holy Spirit that this child has been conceived in her. She will bear a son and you are to name him Jesus, because he will save his people from their sins." — Matthew 1:18–21*

Joseph is something of a mystery. Though he was chosen by God to be the earthly father of Jesus, very little is said about him in the Bible, and so there is very little we can know for certain.

We don't know his age at the time he got married or what his personality was like. Nothing is known for certain about when or how he died. Not a single word he uttered was memorialized by the Gospel writers.

Here's what we do know about this important man:

- We know that Joseph was born into the lineage of David and that his family came from Bethlehem.
- We know that he was a skilled laborer who worked with his hands. Tradition calls Joseph a carpenter, but the Greek word used by Matthew and Mark is *tekton*, which can also be translated as mason or metallurgist, so either is a possibility.
- We know that he was an honorable man unwilling to subject Mary to scorn, derision, or punishment for the apparent sin of becoming pregnant.

And we know that Joseph was a dreamer. There are four of his dreams recorded in the Gospel of Matthew. Today's story is set during the second of the four dreams. And in every case, the story follows the same pattern: First, God has something to communicate in order to accomplish His will. Then, He sends an angel to speak to Joseph in his dream. Finally, Joseph wakes up and promptly obeys the requests made in the dream without hesitation or question.

Think about that for a moment: Every single time an angel appeared to Joseph, he listened and then obeyed — without questioning or hesitating. This shows just how close to the Lord Joseph was. I know that in my own life, when I have an experience of God in prayer, it takes quite a bit of discernment on my part (and often in consultation with others I trust) before I feel confident that I understand what God is trying to say and what He is asking of me. Joseph didn't need that. Matthew indicated that Joseph's action was immediate, which tells me that Joseph was confident that the dream really came from God and that he should act on it. He knew what God's voice and the voice of His messenger sounded like. He was sure.

Joseph also had enough confidence in himself to trust that God was speaking to *him*. Even though he was married to the Immaculate Conception herself, the spouse of the Holy Spirit, he trusted that God could still work through him.

We want Joseph's level of faith and his rootedness in his identity for our own children. We want them to recognize God's voice, His message, His truth when they hear it. Most of all, we want them to be confident in who they are as His children.

CONVERSATION STARTERS

- How do you think Joseph knew to trust the dream?

- Do you think you would have trusted if you were in his place?

- Why do you think God spoke to Joseph instead of Mary?

December 16 • Mary

Mary touched her stomach gently. Wonder filled her whole being, from the tip of her head right down to her toes. She had been chosen to be the mother of the Savior! She felt overwhelmed by the blessing and the responsibility — raising the Messiah, feeding Him, loving Him, keeping Him from harm, teaching Him — but she knew that the Spirit of God had overshadowed her when the angel Gabriel appeared to her. That same Spirit now spoke softly to her, reminding her that she would not be left alone.

As she listened to that gentle voice, she knew that whatever came next, she would always answer yes when God asked.

Read Mary's full story in the Gospel of Luke, beginning with chapter 1.

Note for Parents

But Mary said to the angel, "How can this be, since I have no relations with a man?" And the angel said to her in reply, "The holy Spirit will come upon you, and the power of the Most High will overshadow you. Therefore the child to be born will be called holy, the Son of God. And behold, Elizabeth, your relative, has also conceived a son in her old age, and this is the sixth month for her who was called barren; for nothing will be impossible for God." Mary said, "Behold, I am the handmaid of the Lord. May it be done to me according to your word." Then the angel departed from her. — Luke 1:34–38

Theologians have speculated and debated for millennia about what Mary knew when she said yes to Gabriel. Interestingly, out of all four of the Gospel accounts, the Gospel of Luke is the only one to provide us with insights into Mary's experiences. Tradition tells us that this is because Saint Luke knew her. How else would he have known about the angel's visit? Think about that: The apostles and other believers in the early Church had the opportunity to ask Mary questions about the birth of Jesus, about His childhood, and about her experiences with her Son.

What an amazing thing that would have been! All of us today can only speculate about what those conversations would have been like, but for my part, I wonder what she was asked, by whom, and how often. What were Peter's questions about his Lord? What did John, the Beloved, want to know as they sat at the dinner table? I wonder whether she loved talking about her Son, or whether she tended toward silence unless prodded into speech. Personally, I suspect it was the latter.

As an author who has done some interviews as part of writing books, I find it very interesting which pieces of information Luke included in his account. When you interview someone, whether it is a formal interview or a more casual conversation, generally you listen to everything, pay close attention, and take copious notes. It's not until later that you pull the pieces of information that are most important or best support your work for inclusion.

So why this scene? Why did Luke include the Annunciation instead of, say, the conversation Mary had with Joseph or the first word Jesus spoke? It's likely that Luke knew much more about Mary's experiences than he shares in his Gospel account.

And yet, he chose this moment. That to me is significant.

I think Luke chose to include stories about Mary that show us what steadfastness looks like. Luke's Gospel doesn't answer the question of what Mary knew. I suspect that this is because he was not concerned with how much she understood about what her Son would suffer or her intellectual understanding of who the Messiah would be.

What did concern Luke was Mary's yes. That single sentence, "May it be done to me according to your word" (Lk 1:38), is the centerpiece of Mary's story in Luke's telling of it. And this is fitting because Mary's fiat changed the world. It was through her yes that God was able to become man.

In each and every moment that we encounter Mary in Luke's Gospel, we see that yes lived out, both internally and externally. We see it at the Nativity, in her welcoming of both the shepherds and the wise men. We see it when Jesus is presented at the Temple and Mary is told that a sword will pierce her heart. We see it when Jesus is lost and then found at that same Temple. We see it at the Wedding Feast at Cana. And we see it at the Crucifixion of her Son. Time and again we find Mary submitting to the divine will, not out of naivete but rather out of faith.

This is what we can model for our children: In order to say yes to God, we do not have to have all the answers; we do not have to understand everything that is happening in the world or even the entirety of our own place within it. The Blessed Mother shows us how to say yes with perfect trust, and she is our help in times of need.

Conversation Starters

- What do you think Mary did after Gabriel left her?

- Do you think she shared the news with anyone?

- What do you think gave Mary the courage to answer yes to God's calling?

O Antiphons

Introduction to the O Antiphons for Kids

For the next several days, we are going to learn about some names for Jesus. These are included in short prayers called the "O Antiphons." For each day, we will read and pray with the passage from the Bible that corresponds with the O Antiphon for the day. The O Antiphons help us better understand who Jesus is and His relationship to us.

Then, on Christmas Eve, we'll listen to Jesus' own words telling us who He is.

Note for Parents on the O Antiphons

The O Antiphons, or Great Antiphons, have been in use in the liturgical life of the Church since at least the eighth century, when we have a record of them being used in the Church in Rome. They are traditionally a part of the Liturgy of the Hours, said before the Magnificat (Mary's great profession of faith to Elizabeth at the Visitation) during Evening Prayer. The O Antiphons are recited from December 17 to December 23. There is no O Antiphon said on Christmas Eve because, according to the tradition of the Church, major feast days begin the evening before, so Evening Prayer on Christmas Eve is actually Evening Prayer I of Christmas.

Each O Antiphon is a title of the Messiah from the Old Testament. Each refers to a prophecy from the Book of Isaiah, and all follow the same pattern: First comes a title of the Messiah; next an explanation of something that God does because of who He is; and last, a prayer asking the Lord to come and give a specific type of help to His people. You might recognize some of the O Antiphons, which are the basis for the verses of the hymn "O Come, O Come, Emmanuel." Short though they are, the O Antiphons contain depth and wisdom, which is why there are no meditations included for these days. This is to encourage you to pray the verses slowly with your children and appreciate the beauty of the words of the Church. In our house we recite the O Antiphons as we light the Advent wreath, usually saying them right before we sing a verse of "O Come, O Come Emmanuel."

Using *Lectio Divina* with the O Antiphons

Instead of conversation starters, I would encourage you to use a modified version of *lectio divina* for these days. The process is very simple.

First, set the stage: ensure that everyone is paying attention and is quiet and peaceful (or as peaceful as small children get). We've found that lighting the wreath first seems to get our kids into the mood to pray.

Next, tell the children that you are going to read from Scripture, and that this is one of the ways we learn to hear God's voice. Ask the children to pay attention to any words that stick out in their minds as they listen.

Then, read the antiphon slowly and prayerfully. For each evening's antiphon, make sure to pause after the first time you read the words and ask your children if they need any of the words explained to them.

Then repeat the O Antiphon again, and follow it with the appropriate verse of "O Come, O Come, Emmanuel" and any other Advent prayers you might wish to say.

Once you finish your time of prayer, you can hang the day's ornament on the tree. You might choose to use this time of hanging the ornament to ask your children what words of the antiphon stuck out to them as particularly important. Because these words come from Scripture, they are living words, words that can cut to the heart. Ask follow-up questions like "Why do you think that word stuck out to you?" "How does this make you feel?" "Does it remind you of anything else you've learned about God?" These kinds of questions can help your child understand what God was trying to say to them in His word.

DECEMBER 17 • O SAPIENTIA (O Wisdom)

Explain that the O Antiphons come from the Bible. They are God's living word and have the power to speak to us today.
Ask your children to pay attention to any words that stand out to them in the passage.
Read the O Antiphon, slowly and prayerfully:

O Wisdom of our God Most High,
guiding creation with power and love:
come to teach us the path of knowledge!

After you've read, ask your children if they need help understanding any of the words. If there was something that they didn't understand, consider reading it again.

CONVERSATION STARTERS

- What word or phrase stuck out to you?
- What did it make you think of? Why?

- How does this O Antiphon make you feel?

- Does it remind you of anything else you've learned about God?

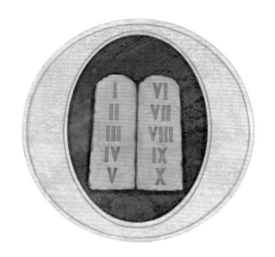

DECEMBER 18 • O ADONAI (O Leader of the House of Israel)

Explain that the O Antiphons come from the Bible. They are God's living word and have the power to speak to us today.
    Ask your children to pay attention to any words that stand out to them in the passage.
    Read the O Antiphon, slowly and prayerfully:

> O Leader of the House of Israel,
> giver of the law to Moses on Sinai:
> come to rescue us with Your mighty power!

After you've read, ask your children if they need help understanding any of the words. If there was something that they didn't understand, consider reading it again.

CONVERSATION STARTERS

- What word or phrase stuck out to you?
- What did it make you think of? Why?

- How does this O Antiphon make you feel?

- Does it remind you of anything else you've learned about God?

DECEMBER 19 • O RADIX JESSE (O Root of Jesse's Stem)

Explain that the O Antiphons come from the Bible. They are God's living word and have the power to speak to us today.

Ask your children to pay attention to any words that stand out to them in the passage.

Read the O Antiphon, slowly and prayerfully:

> *O Root of Jesse's stem,*
> *sign of God's love for all His people:*
> *come to save us without delay!*

After you've read, ask your children if they need help understanding any of the words. If there was something that they didn't understand, consider reading it again.

CONVERSATION STARTERS

- What word or phrase stuck out to you?
- What did it make you think of? Why?

- How does this O Antiphon make you feel?

- Does it remind you of anything else you've learned about God?

December 20 • O Clavis David (O Key of David)

Explain that the O Antiphons come from the Bible. They are God's living word and have the power to speak to us today.

Ask your children to pay attention to any words that stand out to them in the passage.

Read the O Antiphon, slowly and prayerfully:

O Key of David,
opening the gates of God's eternal kingdom:
come and free the prisoners of darkness!

After you've read, ask your children if they need help understanding any of the words. If there was something that they didn't understand, consider reading it again.

Conversation Starters

- What word or phrase stuck out to you?
- What did it make you think of? Why?

- How does this O Antiphon make you feel?

- Does it remind you of anything else you've learned about God?

December 21 • O Oriens (O Radiant Dawn)

Explain that the O Antiphons come from the Bible. They are God's living word and have the power to speak to us today.
  Ask your children to pay attention to any words that stand out to them in the passage.
  Read the O Antiphon, slowly and prayerfully:

> *O Radiant Dawn, splendor of eternal light, sun of justice:*
> *come and shine on those who dwell in darkness and in the*
> *shadow of death.*

After you've read, ask your children if they need help understanding any of the words. If there was something that they didn't understand, consider reading it again.

Conversation Starters

- What word or phrase stuck out to you?
- What did it make you think of? Why?

- How does this O Antiphon make you feel?

- Does it remind you of anything else you've learned about God?

December 22 • O Rex Gentium (O King of All Nations)

Explain that the O Antiphons come from the Bible. They are God's living word and have the power to speak to us today.

Ask your children to pay attention to any words that stand out to them in the passage.

Read the O Antiphon, slowly and prayerfully:

O King of all nations and keystone of the Church:
come and save man, whom You formed from the dust!

After you've read, ask your children if they need help understanding any of the words. If there was something that they didn't understand, consider reading it again.

Conversation Starters

- What word or phrase stuck out to you?
- What did it make you think of? Why?

- How does this O Antiphon make you feel?

- Does it remind you of anything else you've learned about God?

December 23 • O Emmanuel

Explain that the O Antiphons come from the Bible. They are God's living word and have the power to speak to us today.

Ask your children to pay attention to any words that stand out to them in the passage.

Read the O Antiphon, slowly and prayerfully:

O Emmanuel, our King and Giver of law:
come to save us, Lord our God!

After you've read, ask your children if they need help understanding any of the words. If there was something that they didn't understand, consider reading it again.

Conversation Starters

- What word or phrase stuck out to you?
- What did it make you think of? Why?

- How does this O Antiphon make you feel?

- Does it remind you of anything else you've learned about God?

DECEMBER 24 • JESUS IS THE LIGHT OF THE WORLD

Jesus spoke to them again, saying, "I am the light of the world. Whoever follows me
will not walk in darkness, but will have the light of life." — John 8:12

The shepherds huddled close to their sheep. The night was cold and dark, but clear. In the sky gleamed thousands of stars. Breathing in and out, they could see their breath coming in puffs. Everything was silent except the sheep. The rest of Bethlehem was asleep, but they kept their watch, waiting for the dawn when light would come.

CONVERSATION STARTERS

- Can you imagine being a shepherd out on a cold night?

- What would you be thinking of as you sat in the cold and dark, keeping your sheep safe?

- What is going to happen next to the shepherds?

About the Author

Colleen Pressprich is the author of *Marian Consecration for Families with Young Children* and *The Women Doctors of the Church*. She is a homeschooling mom of five who lives with her husband, kids, and mom in Michigan. As a former missionary and former Montessori teacher, she seeks to use the lessons learned in the mission field and the classroom to live her dream of growing her domestic church and helping other families to do the same.

About the Illustrator

Amy Heyse is a Catholic artist who lives in Fort Collins, Colorado, with her husband, two daughters, and cat. Her favorite way to connect to God is through creating, and she loves to make artwork inspired by her prayer life. She has worked as a painting instructor for the past ten years and enjoys teaching artists of all ages. When she's not working on art, she loves watching movies and reading while snuggled up in her favorite bathrobe. You can learn more about her work at amyheyse.com.